YOUR KNOWLEDGE HAS VALUE

- We will publish your bachelor's and master's thesis, essays and papers

- Your own eBook and book - sold worldwide in all relevant shops

- Earn money with each sale

Upload your text at www.GRIN.com and publish for free

Rhianmôr Thomas

How the Removal of Cherokee Children from Tsalagi Speaking Homes Led to a Decline in the Tsalagi Language

A Research Dossier

GRIN Verlag

Bibliografische Information der Deutschen Nationalbibliothek:

Die Deutsche Bibliothek verzeichnet diese Publikation in der Deutschen National-
bibliografie; detaillierte bibliografische Daten sind im Internet über http://dnb.d-
nb.de/ abrufbar.

Imprint:

Copyright © 2009 GRIN Verlag GmbH
Druck und Bindung: Books on Demand GmbH, Norderstedt Germany
ISBN: 978-3-656-37347-6

This book at GRIN:

http://www.grin.com/en/e-book/208802/how-the-removal-of-cherokee-children-
from-tsalagi-speaking-homes-led-to

GRIN - Your knowledge has value

Der GRIN Verlag publiziert seit 1998 wissenschaftliche Arbeiten von Studenten, Hochschullehrern und anderen Akademikern als eBook und gedrucktes Buch. Die Verlagswebsite www.grin.com ist die ideale Plattform zur Veröffentlichung von Hausarbeiten, Abschlussarbeiten, wissenschaftlichen Aufsätzen, Dissertationen und Fachbüchern.

Visit us on the internet:

http://www.grin.com/

http://www.facebook.com/grincom

http://www.twitter.com/grin_com

C O N T E N T S

P R O J E C T   D O S S I E R

Introduction   p2

The Missionaries and "Civilisation"   p3

Henry Richard Pratt and the Carlisle Indian Industrial School   p5

Sequoyah and His Syllabary   p7

Effects and Decline in Language and the Solutions   p9

Bibliography   p12

Between the Franco- Indian War, and the American Revolution, settlers in the United States began to push westward (Green & Perdue, 2005, p6) under the justification of Manifest Destiny, which was the belief that it was the settlers' divine right to expand westward. (Bailey, 1991, p363) Settlers began to encroach on Cherokee territory which created competition for food. However, the King's Proclamation of 1763 forbade settlement anywhere west of the Appalachian Mountains. Unfortunately, settlers ignored this proclamation since it could not be strictly enforced by the British Government. Due to this invasion of territory, the Cherokee tribes began to regard these settlers as an enemy. As a result, the Cherokee nation sided with the British during the American Revolution as the British had tried to prevent the colonisation of settlers on Cherokee land. (Green & Perdue, 2005, p6).

The Treaty if Hopewell, signed in November, 1785, was intended almost as a peace treaty, defining the boundaries of Cherokee land to Georgian and North Carolinian settlers. (Jefferson, 2007, p139) However the settlers proceeded to ignore this treaty and continued to encroach on Cherokee land. (Green & Perdue, 2005, p9)

During the summer of 1776, during the American Revolution, the colonies invaded and most Cherokee captives were executed instantly. Treatment of the Cherokees got so brutal during this time that rewards were being offered for the scalps of Indian warriors. By the end of the American Revolution, the colonists had destroyed over fifty towns, Cherokees had surrendered more than twenty thousand square miles of their land, and the Cherokee population had declined dramatically, mainly because of epidemics and starvation. (Green & Perdue, 2005, p7).

The Peace of Paris, signed in 1784, signified the end of the American Revolution and the United States was now independent. This independence presented claims to the land within its boundaries,

including the lands that belonged to the Cherokee Nation. (Green & Perdue, 2005, p7). At the end of the 1780's the US Government underwent a reorganisation. This reorganisation placed sole authority over Indian affairs and territory in the hands of the President and Congress, (Prucha, 1997, p157) as many felt that people who were "uncivilised" had no right to land. (Perdue & Green, 2007, p12)

The Missionaries and "Civilising" the Indians

Henry Knox, the secretary of war at that time, and President George Washington presumed that Native Americans would assimilate to American society, as equal citizens, once they had been "civilised" (Green & Perdue, 2005, p15). In this context "civilised" meant being a part of the existing contemporary American culture. It was believed by Knox and Washington, that Indians were "uncivilised" because they didn't know any better. (Green & Perdue, 2005, p11). Racism arose, bringing with it arguments that Native Americans could never be fully "civilised". This claim was also used during a congressional debate in 1830 to rationalise the removal of the Indians. President Andrew Jackson signed 'The Indian Removal Act' on May 28th, 1830 which began the Trail of Tears. [Figure 1] (Perdue & Green, 2005, p15) Jackson claimed the Indian Removal Act to be a compassionate action, but the Cherokee did not see it that way. They challenged the Act in the Supreme Court; however, in Cherokee Nation vs. Georgia in 1831, the Supreme Court refused to hear the case as the Cherokee Nation did not embody a sovereign nation. (Cherokee-nc.com)

"...The Indians do not know what is best for them...like children they have to be guided." - Andrew Jackson, Public Address on the Removal Act. (Perdue & Green, 2005, p126)

Eventually the term "civilised" expanded to include Christian practises, a formal education and a Republican Government. (Perdue & Green, 2005, p26) Missionaries came and established stations to accomplish these goals. They set up schools for Cherokee children to educate them about the American culture to which they should be adapting. (Green & Perdue, 2005, p45)   These missionaries looked to convert the children, and as a later effect, the adults. They found that the mixed blood children were more willing to accept this new culture than the full blooded children were. The full blooded children were unable to understand the words and new concepts. (Ehle, 1988, p136) In order to help the children adapt faster and more easily they had to be separated from their culture, and by direct correlation, their families. They were forced to live in dormitories at the missions, or with mission families. Their activities were very closely supervised; the children all learned to read, write and pray in English. They were instilled with the idea that "civilisation" was preferable to their traditional culture. (Perdue & Green, 2005, p46)

In the early 1800's, R. J. Meigs recorded a few social movements occurring amongst Cherokees. The first was a spread of Christianity, although the numbers were still fairly small. The second was the nature of white culture challenging the everyday ways of Cherokee culture, especially concerning raising their children. (Ehle, 1988, p94)

Henry Richard Pratt and the Carlisle Indian Industrial School

The Carlisle Indian Industrial School was intended to raise the Cherokee children "correctly" and was founded by Henry Richard Pratt. Henry Richard Pratt was born in Rushford, New York in 1840. By the end of the American Civil War, Pratt had worked his way up from Corporal to Captain in the Union Army. After the end of the Civil War, he enlisted in the regular army. Given the role of First Lieutenant and assigned to the Tenth Cavalry, he was allocated to Fort Gibson in the Indian Territory for eight years. It was during these eight years, that Pratt observed the Indian way of life and formed his personal opinion on them. (digital.library.edu) Pratt decided neither the Cherokees, nor any other Native Americans should be allowed to run their own schools, or to control the upbringing of their children. (Witte & Mero, 2008, p4)

The Carlisle Indian Industrial School was founded by Henry R. Pratt on November 1st, 1879. (Nelson, 2007, pB12) Pratt's military experience provided him with the model on which he chose to base his educational establishments. (Pratt had also opened a similar institute at Fort Marion.) He structured the schools much like he had structured a prison school Pratt had created years before, for Indian prisoners of war, in Florida. His philosophy on these structures was that unyielding order was the best option and these structures were used in many other Indian boarding schools. Children as young as the age of five were taken away from their families and placed in the intense disciplinary environment that was believed to be necessary. Punishment was frequent in Carlisle, for displaying any Native American habits. (Pember, 2007) The children were given "proper" clothes and the boys' hair was cut. (Centralpa.org)

Children began English lessons almost immediately after arrival and were forced to select Anglo names to replace their Indian ones. The destruction of their native languages was one of Pratt's main objectives because he believed that "civilisation" lay in the language. Once they had learned English, they would be open to the new (contemporary American) culture. (Centralpa.org) Pratt described his mission as "...Kill the Indian and save the man..." (Britannica Encyclopedia Online)

The punishments were sometimes severe if the children spoke in their native tongues, even in private. They could be beaten, have their mouths scrubbed out with lye soap or be forced to forfeit meals. (Centralpa.org) There is a cemetery which holds 186 graves of students that died while attending Carlisle. (Witte & Mero, 2008, p401)

> "...They didn't let the students speak in the old language. It's dying out. The whole spirituality and way of thinking is intertwined with the language..." – Hollow Horn (Centralpa.org)

By cancelling out the native languages, Pratt hoped to also cancel out their native cultures, replacing them with "civilised" culture. Pratt's application of Americanisation of Native Americans, especially the children, by forcing them into cultural assimilation as demonstrated at Carlisle, was later regarded as a form of cultural genocide. (Witte & Mero, 2008, p384)

Unfortunately it was not just a cultural death that was occurring. By 1900, the American Indian population north of Mexico dropped from its original 3 million to around 400, 000, a large amount of which were Cherokees. The cause of this decline in population ranged from disease epidemics brought in by the settlers, to the deaths of Indian warriors who had fought in the American Revolution. The presence of European settlers greatly impacted not just the language and culture, but also the mortality rates, drastically altering the Indian Nation. (Stotter, 1999, p60)

SEQUOYAH AND HIS SYLLABARY

However, a paradox to this massacre of language was the Cherokee syllabary invented by Sequoyah. Sequoyah was a Cherokee Indian born in 1776, in present day Tennessee. (Waxman, 2004, p6) He also held the name George Gist, given to him by his white father. However his father left the Cherokee community before his son was born. (Klausner, 1993, p5)

Sequoyah first became interested in the written word as he became a silversmith when he moved to Georgia. The art of being a silversmith required him to sign his works. (BBC Online) Since Sequoyah didn't know how to write he sought out Charles Hicks, a wealthy farmer in the area who could write in English. Hicks showed Sequoyah how to spell his name by writing down the letters for him. (Geocities.com) In 1808 the Cherokee legal code was set down in written form, demonstrating the effect Sequoyah's syllabary was going to have on Cherokee culture. (Yenne, 1986, p36)

Around the same time, Sequoyah was considering the idea of a Cherokee writing system. This idea of the importance of a written language system within a culture had been reinforced by his experience in the Creek War where he got to observe American soldiers using codes and writing letters. (BBC Online)

For years Sequoyah worked to perfect his Cherokee Syllabary. Once he had a set of letters, he taught it to his six year old daughter Ahyoka. He would show her the writing and she would read the sentence out loud. This proved to him and others that his syllabary really did work and could be taught like any other written language. (Ehle, 1988, p160) Sequoyah's Syllabary started with around two hundred letters. (Waxman, 2004, p31) Eventually he reduced this to eighty five letters. (Yenne, 1986, p36) He perfected this system around 1921. (Bender, 2002, p25)

Sequoyah's syllabary was accepted into the Cherokee culture, but the missionaries had conflicting views on this new development. On the one hand, this new syllabary could have assisted the desired conversion of Cherokees to Christianity. Whereas some feared that it would interfere with the missionaries' efforts to teach English, for now there was a way to read and write in Tsalagi. (Bender, 2002, p23) This advancement in the Cherokees' native language could either help to "civilise" them or further isolate them from the missionaries and Christianity. (Bender, 2002, p31)

In 1824, the Eastern council voted Sequoyah a medal for his contribution to the Cherokee culture and language, despite the fact that he and his family had moved to Arkansas that year. (Ehle, 1988, p304) Sequoyah died in 1843 of disease, but preserved a part of the Cherokee culture from destruction, by finally giving the Tsalagi language a source of survival. (Waxman, 2004, p43) In 1828 the Cherokee Phoenix, the first bilingual newspaper to write articles in Tsalagi and English, began printing, providing another cultural milestone for the Cherokee Nation. (Waxman, 2004, p36) However in 1834, the Georgia Guard destroyed the printing press in the offices of The Cherokee Phoenix as an attempt to prevent progress for the Tsalagi language. (crystallinks.com) From a culturally traditionalist point of view, Sequoyah's syllabary helped preserve the language that missionaries were trying to eradicate from their culture. (Bender, 2002, p39)

Effects and Decline in Language and the Solutions

The Cherokee Nation is currently the second largest Indian tribe in the United States and they control approximately sixty-six thousand acres of land. Today, around twenty two thousand people speak Tsalagi, mainly in Oklahoma and North Carolina. Although it is a more widely spread language than many other Native American languages, it is still endangered as a language due to government policies as late as the nineteen fifties, which enforced removal of Cherokee children from Tsalagi speaking homes. This reduced the number of Cherokee children being raised bilingually. Originally it was at around seventy-five percent of the Cherokee population, whereas today it is just under five percent. (Native-languages.org)

The decline in the Tsalagi language is mainly due to an outstretched process of acculturation, where Cherokee children were forced to adopt the behaviour patterns of the European cultures. This refers in particular, to the trend of Federal boarding schools modelled after Pratt's Indian Industrial School in Carlisle. (Harbold, 2005, p36-37) This created an aftershock effect, as today's older Cherokee speakers came of age at a time where children could be beaten for speaking Tsalagi. Many of this generation felt it was injudicious to teach their own children to speak their native language. (Williams, 1995, p113) This removal led to a decline of fluency in two generations of the Cherokee Nation.

Cherokee children are often still removed from their homes as state courts may define them as "dysfunctional" under the basis of European-American cultural norms. Cherokee police officers try to be the first responders in such incidents. They often have tribal officers present, as Indian Child Welfare Workers have stated that knowledge of traditional Cherokee family structures and social systems are different, therefore they do not necessarily fall under the same laws. If Cherokee children were routinely taken away from their native speaking homes even today, then the fluency in the Tsalagi language could continue to suffer. (Harvard Online)

Fortunately, there are still many attempts to fully resurrect the Cherokee language, especially in schools. In the 1970's, a bilingual education program was started at tribal schools. This program aimed to teach Cherokee children the syllabary. In the process of setting up this program, some of the teachers also learned the syllabary, extending knowledge across the generations. (Bender, 2002, p50)

By the late 1980's, language classes were being reintroduced into kindergarten through the second grade. In the mid 1990's this was extended so that the syllabary was taught from kindergarten through to high school, and adult classes were also made available. (Bender, 2002, p51) Another movement was underway in the late 1990's to increase the amount of Cherokee language instruction even more, broadening to include adults as well. (Bender, 2002, p55)

Fortunately today there are still Tsalagi speakers who feel more comfortable speaking Tsalagi than English, proving that the language is not lost, simply diminished. (Bender, 2002, p41) Even in 2009, the efforts to revive the Cherokee native language are huge. For instance the curriculum has developed to provide schools, within the fourteen county areas that make up the Cherokee Nation, with all the materials needed to effectively teach their students the Cherokee language. The Cherokee Nation Resource centres in these areas also provide services such as free translators and interpreters to encourage the communities to learn their native tongue. Scholarships are also offered for students to schools such as Harvard, Dartmouth and other Ivy League colleges. For example, Robert Humble, from a Cherokee community in

Oklahoma, received a scholarship for $125,000 for Harvard Business School. Candidates for these scholarships are evaluated on academic excellence, but also a commitment to American Indian culture and community. This sort of opportunity can encourage Native American children to take a deep interest in their culture, and also encourage them to learn their native languages, which in turn could lead to an increase in native Tsalagi speakers, putting the language back on its feet. (Cherokee Nation Online)

Overall despite attempts by missionaries and institutes such as Pratt's, the Tsalagi language did not become extinct as they had wished. The removal of children from their native speaking homes had a great impact on the language and certainly led to a noticeable decline in Tsalagi and a fear to learn. However over the last century, and especially the last few decades, the Cherokee Nation has put great effort into re-educating its citizens. By making the language accessible and a mandatory class in schools, the numbers of fluent speakers has once again begun to rise, allowing the language to start returning to its former place at the centre of Cherokee culture. The destruction the settlers caused is slowly being reversed ,but the impacts it had on the Tsalagi language, people and culture will forever be felt.

"...To all Native American people, every creature and part of the earth was sacred; it was their belief that to waste or destroy nature and its wonders is to destroy life itself. Their words were not understood in their time. Now they have come true and before it is too late, we must listen." – Susan Jeffers (Jeffers, 1991, p29)

BIBLIOGRAPHY

1. ANDERSON, STEPHANIE. (2000). *On Sacred Ground.* [online] Available: http://www.centralpa.org/archives/00maysacred.html. Last accessed 4 April 2009

2. ANON. (2009). *Cherokee Nation Cultural Resource Center.* Available: http://www.cherokee.org/Culture/Language/Default.aspx. Last accessed 25 March 2009.

3. ANON. (2009). *Cherokee Nation Timeline.* Available: http://www.crystalinks.com/cherokee2.html. Last accessed 8 April 2009.

4. ANON (2009) *Native American.* [online] Available: http://www.britannica.com/EBchecked/topic/1357826/Native-American. Last accessed 2 April, 2009.

5. ANON. (1997). *Native Languages of the Americas: Cherokee (Tsalagi).* [online] Available: http://www.native-languages.org/cherokee.htm. Last accessed 12 March 2009.

6. BAILEY, THOMAS A. (1991). *The American Pageant.* 9th ed. Lexington: Wadsworth.

7. BENDER, MARGARET (2002). *Signs of Cherokee Culture.* 1st ed. Chapel Hill: University of North Carolina Press.

8. COATES, JULIA. (2002). *Honouring Nations.* Available: http://www.hks.harvard.edu/hpaied/hn/hn_2002_history.htm. Last accessed 8 April 2009.

9. EHLE, JOHN (1988). *Trail of Tears: The Rise and Fall of the Cherokee Nation.* 1st ed. New York: Anchor Books

10. FRAUST, M., LATINI, S., McWEENEY, K., MOYER, K. M., TURNER, L. & VALDES-DAPENA, A. (2004). *Visualising a Mission*. 1st ed. Carlisle: Dickinson College.

11. GOLDEN, RANDALL L. (1994). *Sequoyah*. [online] Available: http://www.geocities.com/Heartland/Hills/1825/page61.html. Last accessed 12 March 2009.

12. HARBOLD, LAURA. (2005). Speaking Across Generations. *Humanities*. v26 (n5).

13. HASLAM, ANDREW. (2001). *Native Americans*. 2nd ed. Chanhassen: Two-Can Publishing.

14. HUSKEY, KELLY. (2008). *Andrew Jackson*. [online] Available: http://www.cherokee-nc.com/index.php?page=64. Last accessed 4 April 2009.

15. JEFFERS, SUSAN. (1991). *Brother Eagle, Sister Sky*. 1st ed. London: Puffin Books.

16. JEFFERSON, THOMAS. (2007). *The Works of Thomas Jefferson*. 4th ed. Berkeley: University of California Berkeley Press.

17. KLAUSNER, JANET (1993). *Sequoyah's Gift: A Portrait of the Cherokee Leader*. 1st ed. New York: HarperCollins.

18. KUETEMAN, K. B. (2005). *He Goes First: The Story of Episcopal Saint David Pendleton Oakerhater*. [online] Available: http://digital.library.okstate.edu/Oakerhater/bio.html. Last accessed 15 March 2009.

19. MERRYJEST, MAUS. (2003). *History of the Cherokee Language*. [online] Available: http://www.bbc.co.uk/dna/h2g2/A1064846. Last accessed 26 March 2009.

20. NELSON, MICHAEL. (2007). Carlisle Indian Industrial School. *Chronicle of Higher Education*. v54 (n6).

21. PEMBER, MARY ANNETTE. (2007). A Painful Remembrance. *Diverse: Issues in Higher Education*. v24 (n21).

22. PERDUE, THEDA & GREEN, MICHAEL D. (2005). *The Cherokee Removal.* 2nd ed. Boston: Bedford.

23. PERDUE, THEDA & GREEN, MICHAEL D. (2007). *The Cherokee Nation and The Trail of Tears*. 1st ed. New York: Penguin Books.

24. PRUCHA, FRANCIS, P. (1997). *American Indian Treaties: The History of a Political Anomaly*. 2nd ed. Berkeley: University of California Press.

25. STOTTER, MICHAEL. (1999). *North American Indians*, 1st ed. London: Anness Publishing Limited.

26. WAXMAN, LAURA H. (2004). *Sequoyah* 1st ed. Minneapolis: Lerner Publications Group.

27. WILLIAMS, MICHAEL A. (1995). *Great Smoky Mountains Folklife*. 2nd ed. Jackson: University Press of Mississippi.

28. WITMEN, LINDA F. (1979). R. H. Pratt 1879 - 1918. *Cumberland County Historical Society Publications*. v10 (n3).

29. WITTE, DANIEL E & MERO, PAUL T. (2008). *Removing Classrooms from the Battlefield*. 1st ed. Provo: Brigham Young University.

30. YENNE, BILL (1986). *The Encyclopedia of North American Indian Tribes*. 1st ed. Greenwich: Arch Cape Press.